The Remote Worker's Guide to Excellence

D1466968

Eryck Komlavi Dzotsi

DEDICATION

To Dieudonne Komlaga Dzotsi, a father who died too soon, and who did not get a chance to see the fruits of his investments in me.

CONTENTS

ACKNOWLEDGMENTS

Thanks to my mom Kafui, my mother Michelle and my sister Emefa for making me into whom I have become.

Thanks to Jonathan Niebch and James Tribue for challenging me in a time of great tribulations to move on to embrace my full potential.

Thanks to Carissa Vega and Emily Gouwens for exemplifying the ultimate managers to a remote working employee, and to Melanie for making working remotely an option for my hiring into IMPAQT.

Thanks to Ashley O'Barto Colaizzi for her hard work. I could not have made it without you, partner!

Thanks to Ivan Stamenov and Dimitar Simovski for making Pittsburgh a home away from home.

Thanks to my small group, my family away from Africa

Thanks to the Comcast Team (Residential and Business) for helping make my remote working life a success.

Thanks to Lauren, Novak, Alyssa, and Christi, the remote working rock stars for being an inspiration to me.

Thanks to Diane Stanek and Ralph Ruggiero for making remote working pains go away through their care.

Thanks to Jamie Keany without whom this book would have never seen the light of day.

Thanks to Jean-March Mensah, a mentor and friend

To Him in whom I find strength and satisfaction.

INTRODUCTION

Remote working, telecommuting, working from home...no matter what you call it, more people are doing it.

According to the International Data Corporation (IDC), 72.2% of the U.S. workforce was "remote" in 2008, and this number will rise to 75.5% or 119.7 million workers in 2013. The forecast continues to project that 35% of the global workforce will be remote by 2013 – more than one in three workers worldwide. This means that today's marketplace demands workers be more efficient and productive in remote working environments. One has to wonder then, what the best way to make working remotely work well is.

The meaning of remote working can diverge based on company policies and market needs. For the purpose of this book, a remote worker is anyone who works for a company in a different geographical area, and spends the majority of the time at home instead of the office.

There is still a stigma attached to working remotely. For example: two leading digital marketing experts, John

Doherty ("Don't hire remote workers") and Wil Reynolds ("Hiring remote full time workers - not for me") blogged about the pitfalls of hiring remote workers. The CEO of a major CRM agency said at a company event "I can never work remotely, because I drive my energy from [being around] people." The message these individuals are communicating is, "I don't think I can succeed working remotely; therefore I don't think you can either." It is true that different people do better in different environments. This book is for those who think they can succeed as remote workers and want to make sure they are making the right decision, and also seek understand how to do it well.

Though much of the information in this book is valuable for any individual working from home, it focuses primarily on telecommuters, or people who almost always work at home, rather than occasionally, such as when the plumber is coming or the kids get an unexpected snow day. Most of the information comes from my own story as a telecommuter and from other telecommuters whom I have had the chance to spend some time with; the rest came from research.

In 2010, I reached a plateau at my then-current job in Orlando, FL. On the advice of friends and coworkers in the company's leadership, James Tribue and Jonathan Niebch, I set out to find a new place to put my talent to work.

Shortly thereafter, I found just such a place. There was only one catch - the job was in Pittsburgh, PA and I lived in Melbourne, FL. I set out to relocate, but just like many homeowners in Florida, I was the proud owner of a house worth less than half the cost it took to build it only four years earlier. Fortunately, we came to an agreement where I would start the job, work remotely to solve the house situation, and then relocate to Pittsburgh.

Before the Great Recession of 2008, I worked as an independent consultant from home. I had some experience working at home, but never in a job where my primary work location was my residence. I had to develop and implement a plan to make things work for both me and the company.

I spoke with friends who worked from home to understand what the best approach would be. I also read several books and blogs to find tips and tricks for success. However, I discovered most of the resources available were tips for affiliate marketing folks or tips for corporations on how to manage remote workers. Very few resources were available for telecommuters. I dove right in trying to learn from my mistakes as I went along, while making adjustments and asking for help when I needed it.

One year later, I have gotten the hang of working remotely. I have not only survived, but I have thrived in this new arrangement. I ended up being nominated for Employee of the Quarter, as well as the 2011 Award for Innovation, not to mention several other recognitions which currently garnish the walls of my home office.

My only regret is that I wish I had a resource like this book to rely on, so I could have made fewer mistakes and had less hassle throughout the process. Because I haven't found one yet, I've decided to share my experiences with you in the hopes that they can benefit you.

We'll start by talking about the things that you need to consider before you begin, along with the pros and cons of working from home. We will then take a look at what your transition period to working from home should look like. We'll also focus on making the most of your image, your work ethic, and your communications skills as a remote worker and overcome objections other may have.

I wish you the best on this endeavor...

God bless you.

1 - WHO ARE YOU - WHEN NO ONE IS WATCHING?

"Who Are You? Who, Who, Who, Who?" - *The Who*
"Know Thyself" – *Pausanias*

In order to succeed at working from home, or any endeavor, for that matter, you have to understand yourself. Working remotely is not for everyone – you have to make sure working remotely is the right fit for you before you start. Here are some questions to ask yourself:

Do you love your job, your career, or the industry?
Is your job something you are doing to pay the bills or is this what you want to do? Your dedication to your craft is going to drag you through the tough times when you're tired, stressed out, distracted, unfocused, or in a bad mood. When other people doubt you, you will find solace in the fact that your work is a calling for you and not just something you just happen to do.

For others, the motivation is a mean to an end. Knowing your job is just a means to an end has the same effect as if your focus to keeping your job is just so you can take care of your family or maintain your lifestyle, or the job has some perks you greatly enjoy. That may be good enough for some people to hang on, but for some it may not be enough to make it through the tough days. There are plenty of jobs to take care of your family, so when push comes to shove, contemplating options may be a more appealing choice than doubling down to make it through the tough days. Clearly understanding the worth of your job keeps you focused during the tough times of unbalance or professional challenges.

What satisfies you and makes you feel validated?

Some things that make people satisfied at work are:

- Compensation (Money)
- Benefits
- Work-Life balance
- Praise and Recognition
- Development and Career Opportunities
- Making a Difference

If you find satisfaction through money, make sure in your negotiations the compensation you get meet or exceed your expectations. You do not want to be on a tough day at home, working on very challenging projects and all that you can think about is that you wish you were making more money than you currently are. If recognition and praise motivate you, make sure you communicate with your manager to understand how feedback is given.

What qualities do you need to succeed?

The qualities you will need to succeed are:

- Drive and passion
- Self-sufficiency and self-motivation
- Excellent project management skills
- Good communication skills
- Organizational and operational skills

- Technological savvy
- Focus and prioritization acumen

Before you jump in, you need to assess some of the elements that are part of this experience you are about to throw yourself into. The sense of freedom you get from working remotely will make you very happy and productive. You will achieve new records in getting things done. You will also be however somewhat "disconnected" from the world back at the office.

One week, I came back from church and parked my car in the driveway. I was stunned when I realized the next time I got into my car was on my way back to church the next Sunday morning. I had spent the whole week at home without any human interaction.

Working remotely means you have to fight the temptation to slack off. In fact, that temptation is one of the hardest issues of remote work. It takes great focus to avoid shopping online, playing with your dog, or watching reality television and soap operas when you should be working.

What turns you on? What turns you off?

Do you love/hate travelling? Do you enjoy/dread meetings? Do you yearn for/avoid crowds? Do you need to know everything, or are you fine with ambiguity? Are you a morning person or a night owl? Knowing the answers to these questions is essential in determining if remote work is right for you. Each job comes with its set of challenges. You have to assess your career needs and attempt to match your personality to them. If you hate your job and the people you are currently working with, moving to a remote working environment is not going to make it better.

Are you energized/drained by being with others?

Some people are extroverts, others are introverts. The simplest definition of these terms is that an extrovert is someone who is energized by being around others, while an introvert's energy is drained from too much human interaction. If you are an extrovert, or think you might be, you may find remote work to be isolating. On the other hand, introverts may thrive, but may fail to get enough human interaction to avoid becoming anti-social. We all need a certain level of human interaction to remain mentally sane. It is up to you to understand what your level of need is. Honestly assessing your level of human interaction needs will go a long way in preparing you for the work from home environment.

The Bottom Line

It is important to stop and take a good long look in the mirror to figure out who you are and what environment you would do best in. Because we cannot fundamentally change who we are, it is important to put ourselves in environments where we can succeed. Make sure a remote work environment is one in which you can succeed. If your assessment of the above components of your persona points you in a direction that signals remote working is not good for you, do not insist and stay in the office.

2 - WHAT IS THE COMPANY ABOUT?

"When in Rome, do as the Romans do" – Unknown

You may be suited for remote work, but is your job or organization too? That is why it's important to talk to your current or future boss and peers to make the right decision. Like it or not, some organizations, bosses, and workers are better suited and more amenable to employees working remotely than others.

Before You Start

During the interview process, or when you decide to go remote, ask the company representatives about their experience with remote workers and how they have fared thus far. Some questions to ask are:

- How many of your employees are currently working remotely?
- What is the highest job title held by an employee working remotely?
- What are some examples of what you were pleased with in your remote employees?
- What are some examples of what you were displeased with in your remote employees?

Other topics to discuss:

- How often should a remote employee report to the office in person?
- What communication tools are used around the office?
- What are the company policies on chat, video chats, forums, etc.?
- What materials are provided to remote workers?
- How does the remote helpdesk work, and how responsive are the support staff?
- How does the company promote the inclusion of remote workers in company events?

Be very sensitive to your employer's priorities. Is this something they already do, or are you the first? How is the company benefitting by letting you work remotely? Understand that not all companies who have remote employees are thrilled about the concept. The more you understand the political environment surrounding the remote working option at your place of employment, the more equipped you will be to make a decision about it.

Do a Tech Check

A survey conducted by the online publication Mashable http://dzotsi.com/OZwTFu shows that telecommuting is becoming more prevalent, that 83% of the people surveyed said they work remotely at least part of the day, and 90% of the respondents considered collaboration software key components to the success of remote teams. Understanding the technological environment of the company will give you a good gauge of the kind of support they offer to remote employees.

Ask about the IT infrastructure. If you have the best internet connection, but the company's upload speed is not high, you will experience difficulties transferring documents and resources in and out of your company IT environment.

Ask about the communication technologies that are used among the employees in and out of the office. If a company tells you "we do not believe in chat programs in the office," you should have some serious concerns about your potential impact as a remote worker.

Make it a point to talk to a member of the IT team or of the helpdesk team to understand these concerns. During the interview process or during the period in which you are contemplating working from home, set up a meeting with someone who works from home for this company or for another company in the same industry to discuss these concerns. If the preceding options are not available, then ask someone who works in any industry.

Tell It Like It Is

In all conversations, you have to be open about your personal challenges and concerns. The seasoned remote worker may tell you this is something you need to worry about, or that is not an issue within this industry or within this company. The more candid answers you bring to the table, the more value you will gather from it. Understanding the challenges the company or similar companies in the industry have had with remote workers will allow you to make sure you don't raise similar issues, but it will also prepare you to deal with them when they do become an issue in the future.

Now that you have assessed the company's support, or lack thereof, to remote employees, you can deduce if this something for you. Can you do it? Should you walk away now or stick it out?

3 - THE BENEFITS AND THE CHALLENGES OF WORKING FROM HOME

"Don't tell, sell!" - Geoffrey James
"You need stuff that sucks to have stuff that's cool." -Beavis and Butthead

There are great benefits to working remotely. Even though there are a lot of myths out there, the real benefits are nonetheless very real. Those benefits, however, come with added risks. Each of the benefits can be a challenge if not managed properly.

Office Space? No Thanks

Your first benefit is you represent to your employer a way to have skillful employees on their payroll without mandating them to be in the office or in a specific geographic area. This means you are more than likely in a situation where you are not a burden to the company. You are also allowing the company to grow without worrying about additional accommodations within the office (space, desk, cubes, etc...). This is critical because when the economy or the company takes a hit, costs are the first places where people cut, and if you cost too much, you will be cut.

Saving Time, Money, and Hassle

You save the time that you would have spent otherwise commuting in and out of the office. People in major urban areas will greatly value this benefit. Gone are the stressful traffic jams and long train/bus rides. You can re-allocate this time to projects or work-life balance. The words "I need to get out of here to avoid traffic," or "I need to leave now to catch the train/bus" will not pass your lips on a daily basis. For those of you who drive, you will save on fuel, maintenance, tolls and other transportation costs associated with the commute. If you are conscious about the environment, you will greatly appreciate the impact, or lack thereof, you are having on the world.

Beating the Clock

When you work from home, you have the responsibility and the ability to push yourself to limits sometimes prohibited in the office. Some people leave the office because they do not want to be the last one in the building, whether they forgot the alarm code (guilty as charged) or for some other reasons. I used the cleaning crew at my last job as the signal to exit the building. I would have a conversation with them enquiring about their well-being and that of their families, and then I would pack up my stuff and leave. You can also work really early or late if you choose to do so more easily than in your cube or your office. The time that you save from the commute can be re-allocated for either planning or catching up on other projects.

Hocus Pocus, Need More Focus

The reduction of distraction and the increase in productivity is greatly amplified. When you are in the office, people would stop by your booth, cube, or office just to chat. Though that is great for culture development and team cohesion, the timing of it is not always welcomed. The great thing about working from home is that very few people (except folks like me) would disrupt you for items unrelated to work, whether through chat, email, or phone. Almost all the communication coming your way from co-workers would have a purpose. This makes it possible for you to have a higher level of focus on your tasks. Without distractions such as foot traffic, other co-workers on the phone or casual conversation you are not part of, you are able to devote your entire attention to your work.

You gain control about your work environment, your setting, and your time. I have a customized desk setup that allows me to reach levels of multitasking many workers can only dream of having in a cube or on an office environment. I also play loud music when I am working on specific projects. Vivaldi and Handel provide soundtracks to my strategy development sessions, whereas Jay Z, Wyclef Jean, and Bob Marley serenade my tactical implementation sessions. Paul Simon and the Soweto Gospel Choir muse my creative writing periods. It would be a great distraction to co-workers if I were to indulge in my musical needs within an office setting, even with ear buds (as I often accidentally hum). The control that you get of your work environment will allow you to achieve levels of productivity you would not obtain as easily otherwise.

You will be able to improve your work life balance and reduce the amount of stress if you manage your time well. This is an important part of success. Your inability to reduce your level of stress, and reaching a degree of work to life balance would make it that your successes are not short fuses, as they will instead be sustained performances.

Your ability to constantly shine and become a rock star within the organization depends on you being successful at getting this right. You first have to understand your own definition of work-life balance.

Staying Balanced, Staying Connected

Don't stop working long hours just because you are told to or because others do. It's all about balance. My scale is not your scale and there aren't always standards. Suppose your company may have a requirement for you to work an average of 45 hours per week. If you sleep 7 hours a night, that leaves you with 74 hours of life as there are 168 hours in a calendar week (120 hours in a work week).

Some people might say that 74 hours (or 40 hours per work week) is more life than work, and some may disagree. If you count the sleep time as part of your life time, the balance tips even more. It is therefore fundamental that you define for yourself what constitutes balance, and it will depend on where you are in your life cycle.

Balance for a 22-year old out of college single woman with no kids is not the same as that of a 46-year old executive who is a mother of two kids and has sick parents to take care of. For some people 40 hours per week is enough. For some others 65 hours is more like the norm. Whichever is best for you and acceptable to your company should be the target for which you strive. Do not adopt someone else's definition of work-life balance, as this is a sure formula towards disaster.

You will be challenged by the fact that despite modern technologies, you will find it difficult to be fully integrated in the team dynamic. Most of the activities that create a stellar team dynamic are often unplanned. Grabbing lunch together, stopping by the water cooler, brainstorming, sharing jokes, and other things that can make your work place more integrated require physical presence. You are often not very immersed in office politics; therefore may not know how to navigate the political minefields and figure out the unwritten rules of your organization. Your best solution here is to develop excellent communication and social skills that will serve you in and out of the office.

The (Not So) Great Escape

For many, the office is often an escape from the troubles at home. The reality is our home lives are not always perfect. Whether you live at home with your parents, with friends, as a couple, or with kids, there are always challenges that often arise. Working from home takes away that escape opportunity in some way.

If you are going through a foreclosure/divorce/illness/name your challenge, it can be challenging to be in the house by yourself (or with others) and not think about these things. Other things such as laundry, home deliveries, and needed errands can constitute additional major distractions. Your ability to draw boundaries between your work hours and your home hours will allow you to overcome this challenge.

4 - YOUR 90-DAY TRANSITION

"Get on the good foot!" - James Brown

So you and your boss have decided that it's in both your interests for you to telecommute. When this happens, it often makes sense to negotiate a plan around a trial period: "I will work from home for 90 days, and we will revisit our arrangements after that time." This gives you the ability to get back into the office if things don't work out. Why 90 days?

Throughout my career, I have read blog posts and business books every time I was promoted or every time I changed jobs, but none of these materials has been as impactful as "The First 90 Days: Critical Success Strategies for New Leaders at All Levels" by Dr. Michael Watkins. The book does not address the remote working aspect of a career, but the principles within it remain true. I have learned the hard way that starting a new job, or making a drastic change to your work environment, requires for optimal success a strategic approach that is holistic and adaptable to the realities of the job function. Before I lay the working from home wisdom in front of you, it is important you understand the principles for success in your first days, no matter where you work. Dr. Watkins' work is anchored on five fundamental propositions:

- "The root causes of transition failure always lie in a pernicious interaction between the situation, with its opportunities and pitfalls, and the individual, with his or her strengths and vulnerabilities (p. 4)."

- "There are systematic methods that leaders can employ to both lessen the likelihood of failure and reach the breakeven point faster (p. 4)."

- "The overriding goal in a transition is to build momentum by creating virtuous cycles that build credibility and by avoiding getting caught in vicious cycles that damage credibility (p. 5)."

- "Transitions are a crucible for leadership development and should be managed accordingly (p. 5)."

- "Adoption of a standard framework for accelerating transitions can yield big returns for organizations (p. 6)."

Work is a series of constant beginnings. You are either, starting on a new project, on a new product, joining a new department, getting a new boss, or being promoted. All beginnings matter in the epic journey we kindly call a professional career. In order to succeed, Dr. Watkins offers a 10-step plan. It is a roadmap structure, so each step will allow you to address a specific challenge within the transition:

- **"Promote yourself:"** a conscientious decision is made that you are entering a new phase of your life. You have to process this change mentally, and align yourself to it. In the case of working from home, this will be the equivalent of telling yourself that you are not working in the office anymore, and you are going to be working from home, and everything that you do from here on has to be done within this new reality.

- **"Accelerate your learning:"** though people will tell you otherwise, nobody has a vested interest in you taking your time to learn the new job. They hired you or promoted you so that you can take on the job as soon as possible. The longer your learning curve takes the more chances you have to falter and fail.

- **"Match strategy to situations:"** there is no rule that works all the time. Even this book that you have in your hands is not a surefire way to success. As its title indicates it is a guide, how you apply that guide to your situation is going to determine your success.

- **"Secure early wins:"** in the first few days, you need to find ways to create personal credibility and develop business value. Try to find easy successes to help you build momentum and establish a track record.

- **"Negotiate success:"** find out how to build a productive relationship with your boss, and once you do that, manage expectations carefully. Working from home, you will quickly find out that your boss is your greatest ally and support. She is also the one whose success is based on yours. Process and internalize that!

- **"Achieve alignment:"** newly hired or promoted individuals often confuse making an early good impression with making change for the sake of making change. You may be tempted to attack the current strategy, but be very careful. If change is needed, align people to the philosophy before you get going. They will follow your leadership, but when things go astray, and they did not believe in your plan in the first place, you'll lose credibility rapidly, and nobody will stand by you.

- **"Build your team:"** it is important that you evaluate your team thoroughly early on, and make adjustments. Some decisions may be tough, but the success of the company and that of your transition are anchored on it.

- **"Create coalitions:"** know the people and the power they carry, whom they influence, and to what they respond. Deliver on that knowledge.

- **"Keep your balance:"** don't lose your ability to make correct judgment calls, whether because of pressure from the new job, or the transition within which you are operating. Find people you can rely on to assess your effectiveness, and listen to them.

- **"Expedite everyone:"** Don't grow alone in the new position. You need to help your bosses, peers, and direct reports to grow quickly as well. It will not only improve your performance, but it will also improve that of the whole organization.

The ultimate plan is for you to build on your own, but allow me to provide you with some key considerations for the development of the said plan.

Set and communicate your goals. Begin with things you want to achieve during the transition and get to work. It is important you set realistic goals for yourself. Make learning the way your company works and how others will be affected by you working remotely instead of in the office a top priority. Understand what stands in the way of your goals and develop a plan to address problems.

Don't hold back from investing in training programs. Your ability to grow new strengths and achieve mastery in the tools and systems required for you to perform your duties will make you a solid rock upon which others can stand.

Make all the strategic connections that will allow you later to be successful at your job. Who are the key players that hold key resources in their hands? The IT team, the data team, the admins, the HR staff, the accounting staff, the CEO's assistant, and your own team should think of you as their "friend" at the end of the 90 days. If they don't feel like they can do you a favor without you asking for it, you are in trouble. Go the extra mile to show your care and show your appreciation for them, because the reality is you will fail without their support.

If you are starting a new job as a remote employee, make sure you spend at least the first two weeks in the office, and then discuss with your boss how often you should return. Negotiate that close to half of your time in your first 90 days is spent in the office if at all possible, but be aware this is an additional cost you are making the company incur. No matter how effective the company's collaboration tools are, they will never replace the personal relationships and connections that are developed by being around other people, especially in the early days.

The first 90 days are the time for you to build a strong sense of belonging and to establish a positive connection with your boss and the whole team. Once you have established trust, your team will go to bat for you. If you have not established a trusting relationship with your key partners within the organization, take whatever measures you need to establish that trust. You will not succeed as a remote employee if you do not have the trust and respect of your team. If within the first three months you are far behind on the points enumerated above, stay in the office.

5 - YOUR WORK ETHIC

"An ethical person ought to do more than he's required to do and less than he's allowed to do" - Bertrand Russell

Why do you work? Is it because you don't have anything else to do? Are you someone who sees work as something you need to do for a paycheck? Is it a calling for you? Or something you merely put up with?

Your work is a testimony of who you are in the workplace, and on that work your evaluation, your credibility, and your legacy will be built. But we live in a culture where work is looked upon as, well, so much work. Attitude towards work is negative as the weekend is celebrated. Terms like "TGIF" or "a case of the Mondays" are symptomatic of this new attitude towards laboring.

As mentioned earlier, one of the greatest challenges of working remotely is the lack of constant interaction and supervision. It's all too easy to succumb to the temptation to do other things when you should be working. Furthermore, when you are at home and unreachable, people may assume that you aren't working.

To overcome these kinds of speculations, your ethics are your greatest asset. While many outcomes are out of your control, your effort is completely in your control. Here are some tips to get control of your work and do right by yourself and your employer.

Set Goals: Make goals daily, weekly, monthly, and achieve them. There is nothing more to it, really. It all comes down to how far you are willing to go to achieve these goals wherever you are. Your willingness to provide very high levels of quality in your performance independently of where you are is at the core of your ability to achieve excellence.

Respond in a timely manner: At the office, people can call or visit you if they need a quick answer. Phone calls, emails, and teleconferences are the only ways people can reach you remotely. That said, it's important to treat remote conversations just as you would in-person conversations. Whether it is the tone of an email, a phone conversation, the prioritization of a project, or the delivery of slides to a presentation on which the entire team is working on, become reliable within your limits, and set proper expectations. After setting the latter, meet them. Build trust with your teammates and your managers, so when there is a delay, the assumption is you are bogged down, not that you are fooling around.

Be professional: Adhere to the same standards at home as those you would if you were in the office. Write like a professional, speak like a professional, and present yourself as a professional. Your team will thank you for it. Despite the growing number of remote employees, the option is still considered a privilege, so do not abuse the opportunity.

Deliver on time: You have to deliver on time with no ands, ifs, or buts. No matter where you work, deadlines are deadlines and you have to meet them. If you are unable to meet them, give ample notice so others who depend on you can plan accordingly.

Maintain Focus: When you're working, work. Avoid distractions in your work environment. Getting up to go grab a snack, checking Facebook, Twitter, or CNN online are time killers that you must watch out for. Be responsible with the time you have. It is not about just putting in the time, it is about doing the work productively.

There is a concept in ethical philosophy known as duty-based ethics. You owe it to everyone you work with to be professional, polished, and punctual, no matter where you work.

6 - YOUR IMAGE

"Clothes make the man. Naked people have little or no influence on society". -Mark Twain

When you think of "professional image," what comes to mind? Business suits? Image consultants? What about telecommuting? People who telecommute talk about how they get to work in their pajamas, sweats, or even their underwear. Sounds like fun, but that's not a good idea.

If you dress sloppy, you are more likely to think and work sloppy. That's why it's important to think about your professional image, even though you're not officially "in the office." Here's how you can improve your professional image as a telecommuter.

Follow the (dress) code. It's important to strike the right balance between being professional and comfortable. By comfortable, that means comfortable for work, not for sleep or for entertainment. Treat your home office with the same respect you would treat a normal office. It helps to dress the same. Most offices these days have a very casual dress code, so it does not require a considerable fashion shift to dress professionally at home. The most important thing is to make yourself comfortable, but do not confuse comfort with unprofessionalism.

Get into the groove. Professional image means more than what you wear. Have the same routine to go to your home office as you would any other office. The more disciplined you are at home, the more natural it feels when you periodically report to the office.

To this effect, you also need to adopt an exit strategy to your workday. A telecommuter I talked to told me that "it is really important to leave the house each day, as I feel better to myself afterwards."

Watch out for background sounds. If you are making a phone call or are in a video teleconference, make sure you have a reasonable degree of quietness around you, and that your kids or pets don't disturb you. Also, if you have any background music, a radio, or TV on, turn them off or mute them.

Let people know if you will be away from your work area. The only way people know you're away from your work are when you telecommute is to set your IM status to "away" or set up an out-of-office alert in Outlook, for example. Don't leave people guessing where you are.

Use common sense. There are dozens of other tips for telecommuters to maintain a positive image, but they all have one thing in common: they all depend on using common sense and good professional judgment.

7 - YOUR COMMUNICATION SKILLS

"Much unhappiness has come into the world because of bewilderment and things left unsaid." - Fyodor Dostoyevsky

The problem that is complained about the most by employers about their telecommuting employees, and one reason why many employers object to telecommuting, is communication. Because you're away from the office, communication is even more important. Here are some important tips to help you communicate better, no matter where you work.

Be available. If you are not available, let others know. Make sure others who depend on you know how and when to best reach you, and let them know if you will be unavailable.

One size does not fit all. Some people prefer emails, others phone calls, still others Skype. It's important to know how others you work with prefer to communicate and honor their preferences whenever possible.

Don't lose track of time zones. You may be working with others in different time zones as a telecommuter. It's important to work out a compromise, be cognizant of time differences, and respect others' time. For example, if you live in New York City, don't schedule a 9:00 AM meeting with people in San Francisco.

It's not just what you say, but also how you say it. Even in non-vocal channels such as email, your tone comes through. The basics of good grammar and professional etiquette apply online and offline.

Don't hide behind a screen. Almost all of your interaction with stakeholders in your organization will be via email, teleconference, IM, Skype, or some other electronic channel. But just because you can use these means of communication does not mean that you should. In some cases, particularly when discussing complex or emotionally charged issues, email and IM are not the appropriate means of communication. In these cases, a phone call or an in-person visit is a better choice.

Keep it simple. Make your communication, no matter what medium you choose, professional, efficient and direct. Don't use big, fancy words when shorter, simpler ones will work.

8 - GOING TO THE OFFICE AND OTHER TRAVEL COMMITMENTS

"I dislike feeling at home when I am abroad" - George Bernard Shaw

Despite modern communication technologies, there is still no substitute for "face time." As a telecommuter, you may be asked to come into the office from time to time, or you may choose to visit your organization's brick-and-mortar location. Here are some reasons why you should give your boss and coworkers some in-person time and how to make the most of that time.

With apologies to David Letterman, here are the Top Ten Reasons to Go to the Office:

#10: To get to know your coworkers, boss, and other VIPs better. It's important that the people you work with get to see the "real you."

#9: To take care of the tools of your trade. Bring your laptop, smart phone, or other gadgets for any needed updates, upgrades, or fixes. Carrying these items with you is easier than shipping them.

#8: To take care of HR issues. If you need to fill out forms, interview people, or take care of other issues, doing so while physically in the office is often much easier.

#7: To meet any new additions to your staff. When new people come on board, it's nice to get to know them in person.

#6: To conduct/receive performance evaluations. If you are responsible for evaluating people, you should conduct evaluations in person. If you are the one receiving an evaluation, it's a really good idea to meet with your boss face-to-face.

#5: To attend critical staff/company meetings. While you can attend these via teleconference, try to make these in person. It's a good way to meet others in your organization and stay abreast of company happenings.

#4: To meet with clients or other external stakeholders. If any clients or other VIPs are in the office, it makes sense to meet them.

#3: To address complex, controversial, or emotionally charged issues. Tough talks are part of organizational life. Having those tough talks in person helps you catch missed nuances, and offer emotional support.

#2: To do fun things with others in your organization. Team building exercises are essential. One thing you should strongly consider is attending your holiday party.

And the #1 reason: Your telecommuting agreement/policy may require it. As mentioned earlier, a key part of making any telecommuting arrangement work is a mutual agreement between you and your boss. That agreement may require you to come in once every month, every other month, or once every quarter. Abide by that agreement.

Some Travel Tips for Telecommuters

There are dozens of books, articles, websites, and other materials out there that talk about how to make business travel less of a hassle, so here are some tips to help.

- Travel very light and only go with the necessary items to the success of your business trip. If you don't need it, don't pack it.

- Make sure you check your bags and handle your luggage properly to avoid lost bags and security hang-ups. Make yourself as comfortable as you can when you travel.

- If finances or budget restrictions are an issue, join airline reward programs. Many of them allow you to check at least one bag for free, and they offer other perks as you gain more status.

- Squeeze in some downtime for other personal activities. Don't leave healthy habits at home. Pack your gym clothes, and visit the hotel fitness center. Eat healthy.

Get into a routine by applying these tips over and over again. Travel is part of any telecommuting arrangement. These tips will help you make the most of your travel experience.

9 - YOU, YOUR TEAM AND BEYOND: BUILD STRONG ALLIANCES

"No man is an island, entire of itself; each is a piece of the continent, a part of the main" - John Donne

Working remotely can be lonely — but it doesn't have to be. Many telecommuters find it hard to build good relationships with their co-workers and stay relevant in multiple cities or locations. Furthermore, many telecommuters find that they feel "out of the loop" and that bonding and establishing trust with their team is difficult, if not impossible. Without camaraderie and trust with those you work with, it can be difficult to be taken seriously. You may suffer from a lack of challenging work, and even raises and promotions will be negatively impacted as a result.

That's the bad news. Though many would not admit it, it is not yet common practice to promote remote employees to higher responsibilities in the organization, especially the positions that require a great deal of people management. As you may recall in Chapter 2, you needed to ask the highest job title held by a remote employee. The answer to that question gives you a good indicator of how high you can go if you work really hard. If the highest position held by remote workers is "account manager," you will have to excel on many levels; often more than your in-office counterparts, to be promoted to the title of "account director."

The good news is that you can build solid relationships and a foundation of trust with your co-workers by following these steps.

Take advantage of what your admins have to offer. In any organization, administrative professionals can be your best allies. Some companies have "Remote Worker Administrators" who specialize in serving telecommuting workers. Admins have the inside scoop when it comes to getting things done, what's going on, and where the real power resides in an organization.

Do good work and do your part. Nobody likes to work with a slacker. Make sure that you submit work on time and to quality standards; know what your role in projects is and who depends on you, and if you need help, ask for it before you're in trouble.

Be social in real life. As a remote worker, you'll often miss many of the non-work-related activities, such as shared meals, volunteer projects, and sporting events which are great opportunities to get to know and be better known by your coworkers. As mentioned earlier, consider making a trip or two into the office, and while you are there, make sure to participate in some of these events. Connecting with and being part of the team is just as important as doing great work.

Don't expect instant camaraderie from everyone. You will not be liked, appreciated, respected or even taken seriously by everyone right away. You can't expect to please everyone, and some people will look at you askance simply because you are a telecommuter. If you can't be best friends, at least try to get along as professionals. Keep in mind that although we find comfort in those who agree with us and support us, we find growth in those who disagree with us and challenge us.

Don't put your social eggs in one basket. Looking forward to seeing the friendly folks from FedEx and the Postal Service? If so, it's time to get out of your house. Try to meet up once or twice a week with colleagues, networking contacts, or friends outside of your home.

Bond with fellow telecommuters. Chances are there are others in your company or community who are telecommuters. There may even be social groups out there for telecommuters. If you can't find such a group, consider starting one.

10 - YOU AND YOUR BOSS

"Management is doing things right; leadership is doing the right things." - Peter Drucker

A good relationship with your boss is the key to your success within the organization. In fact, the number one reason why people leave jobs, sometimes unconsciously, is a poor relationship with their bosses. You depend on your boss for connection to the rest of the organization, setting priorities, getting information, and securing resources; and your boss depends on you to be cooperative, reliable, and trustworthy.

Management goes both ways: it's important to manage your boss, just as it's important for your boss to manage you. Here are seven tips for you to manage your relationship with your boss.

Get to know your boss inside out. Having a good relationship with anyone means getting to know that person. When it comes to your boss, ask yourself: What are her priorities? What drives him crazy? What does she really appreciate? Is he or she:

- Big picture or detail-oriented?
- Focused on results or processes?
- Extroverted or introverted?
- Facts- or feelings-driven?
- Hands-on or laissez-faire?

Don't know? Well, go ask and find out.

Get feedback early and often. Many bosses often are busy, and have other priorities than giving you feedback. That's why it's important to ask for it. Some bosses are better than others at providing feedback; but no matter how your boss approaches feedback, it's important to get that feedback so you can improve or continue on with what works well. Yes, it can be scary sometimes to get feedback, but so is being fired out of the blue.

Don't just come with problems, bring solutions. Bosses are busy and under a lot of pressure. Don't expect your boss to solve all of your problems. If you have a problem, at least begin by solving it yourself. When you come to your boss with a problem, come with an idea for solving it.

Manage expectations and communicate them. Under-promise and over-deliver. Don't just assume you know what the boss expects. Find out. Don't avoid difficult conversations. Be forthright about good and bad news.

Having a problem with your boss? Look in the mirror first. You own half of your relationship with your boss, and you are one hundred percent in control of your own behavior. If your boss is micromanaging you, could it be that you need extra supervision? If your boss criticizes you, could it be that your work could be better? If your boss dismisses your ideas and suggestions, might you need to come up with better ones?

Respect your boss. While there are excellent, great, OK, bad, and terrible bosses, on average, bosses got where they are because they did a better-than-average job in the trenches, earned degrees, showed initiative, demonstrated the ability to motivate people, knew the right people, and networked well. Your boss is your boss for a reason; respect your boss as a person and respect that person's role as your boss.

As a telecommuter, you need to make the case to your boss that you add value, even though you're not in the office. Your boss has to make the case to upper management that it makes sense for you to telecommute. Building solid relationships and bringing in results is the best way to make the case.

11 - YOUR WORK ENVIRONMENT

"A place for everything, and everything in its place." - Benjamin Franklin

Your environment affects you in ways that are very subtle but deep. As a telecommuter, you are fortunate in that you aren't in the cube farm nightmare popularized by so many Dilbert comics. However, you face many other challenges in creating a comfortable and safe workspace that's conducive to productivity.

There is a geographical psychology associated with places in our lives. We act differently in different places. That's why you need to create a comfortable, safe, user-friendly work space where you can perform at your best.

When it comes to setting up your office away from the office, safety and comfort are essential. Here's how to make your work space safe and comfortable.

Safety first. Your work space must, first and foremost, be safe. Important safety tips are:
- Check that your desk and chair are conducive to good posture.

- Adjust the resolution on your monitor, or use a larger monitor, to avoid eye strain.
- Take frequent breaks from typing.
- Whenever possible, use your desktop or laptop PC instead of your tablet or smart phone for reading documents.
- Use surge protectors, and make sure your home's electrical system can handle any equipment you are using.
- Make sure you have the appropriate safeguards in place to protect your company's private information, from using strong passwords to locking your file cabinets.

Get in the comfort zone. Your work space must be comfortable. Here's how to make your work space comfortable and productive too:

- Make sure the area is open, and does not contain many distractions.
- Always make sure your work space is clean either at the end of the day or at the beginning.
- Take a few minutes to clear the area around you so your work space has a good "feel" to it.
- Keep your work space clutter-free and trash-free.
- If you choose, you may listen to background music, but choose music that isn't too distracting.

Good boundaries make good telecommuters. As mentioned earlier, setting boundaries is important to having a smoothly-running professional and personal life. It's therefore important to set those boundaries and communicate them to others in your home.

Dedicate a room, or an area of your living accommodations (house, apartment, loft, trailer, yurt, geodesic dome, you name it) as your workspace and treat it as that. Try not to eat, sleep, watch TV, play games, or do any non-work-related activities there, at least not when you're working.

The boundaries you set go beyond the physical — they extend to your schedule and availability. Set a work schedule and stick to it. Without the discipline of a schedule, it's too easy to fall into the trap of sleeping extra hours in the morning and trying to make up for it by working late, and then you decide that night you'll make up the hours later that week... For the night owls amongst us, the problem is reversed. Because sleep is of no value to you, you may be tempted to overwork and not set boundaries for when to stop. This will have negative impacts on your health and wellbeing.

Your friends who live in the same area as you may think that you're not at work when you work at home. Be clear with them that you are not to be interrupted at home while you're working any more than you should be if you were at the office. You might need to tell people that you are not available to play with your kids, feed the neighbor's dog, or do chores around the house when you are on the clock.

I spoke to a veteran telecommuting mom about her experience. Her policy is that when she's at work, her family is to, in her words, "pretend that she is not at home." She does not even allow anyone who has the day off (spouse or kids) to be at home during her work time. Her office is away from the main living area, and she even keeps her pets away from her work area so they don't distract her. Her family knows that while she's working, she is not available to do anything non-work-related.

By making your work space safe and comfortable, and by setting clear boundaries with your time and space, you're setting yourself up for successful telecommuting.

12 - YOUR EQUIPMENT AND CONNECTIVITY

"A tool is but an extension of the hand, and a machine is but a complex tool." - Henry Ward Beecher

Even the most skilled workers are helpless with no tools, with the wrong tools, or with broken or poor quality tools. To do your best work, you need the best tools you can get.

As a telecommuter, the tools of your trade include laptop/desktop PCs, cellular phones, landline phones, FAX machines, and other devices such as printers, scanners, and tablets. Other tools of your trade include your desk, chair, lamps, and office supplies.

Sometimes, your employer supplies some or all of these tools. Other times, you supply your own tools. Still other times, your employer supplies basic tools and you have the opportunity to enhance or upgrade these tools.

Poor equipment not only hurts your productivity, it also frustrates you. Even the best tool is useless if it breaks often. Often times, an older or slower tool that works reliably is better than the newest, fastest tool that keeps breaking. Furthermore, being away from the office adds a level of complexity and difficulty, as your IT department is not just a phone call away. Problems that would be resolved at the office in minutes often take days to solve for telecommuters.

Although glitches are a part of life, and the tools you have at your disposal may be what you have to work with, even though you wished you had better tools, there are some important best practices to keep in mind in selecting and using the tools of your trade. Here are some of these best practices:

Check up on your company's infrastructure. Companies' infrastructure ranges from excellent to marginal. When you are considering a telecommuting arrangement, ask your IT department about their infrastructure, what the technical limitations of the company are for remote workers, and how the known issues are addressed. In some cases, companies have a great deal of experience supporting telecommuters' needs; in others, telecommuting is the exception, rather than the rule. Keep these contingencies in mind and prepare accordingly.

Work out a system for repairs. Some companies may want you to ship broken equipment to them, while others may send a local representative to your home to make repairs. Find out how the process for repairing equipment works at your organization before you need to use it. Also, as mentioned earlier, your trips to the office are good opportunities to have issues with your equipment taken care of.

Invest in the best connectivity. If you are not

connected, you cannot work. Don't settle for the basic package with your Internet service provider — upgrade to the fastest connection you can get. Even though you'll pay a bit more, you'll be glad you did. If your Internet speed is slow, your upload and download speeds will suffer. Even basic tasks such as reading emails will be hard to do with a slow connection. Make sure you have the fastest upload and download speeds possible, because many "fast" internet connections have fast download speeds, but not-so-fast upload speeds. If you are unsure, ask your internet service provider. Security measures such as firewalls can slow down your connection, so keep in mind data will be downloaded at a much lower speed than the "advertised" speed of your connection. Make sure you understand the requirements and the challenges of your VPN or other login systems too. Finally, strongly consider investing in a cell phone that has Wi-Fi tethering capabilities, if your company doesn't provide one, as it can prove invaluable when the "regular" Internet connection fails.

Back things up, and have a plan for when things go wrong. An uninterruptible power supply is a good investment that will keep you up during power outages. Make sure that vital equipment such as your modem, your router, and other machines are supplied with a backup system. Back up and save your important documents and files regularly.

Don't forget to have a backup plan (or better yet, several plans) to stay connected if you can't work in your home office for any reason. In my case, there's a coffee shop with a semi-private area that's just a 12-minute drive from my house. I also have a Wi-Fi tethering 4G cell phone that I can turn into a mobile Wi-Fi hotspot if I need it.

Don't forget about your low-tech equipment.

Invest in quality desks and chairs. These two items can mean the difference between a comfortable and a tiring work day — and your long-term health. Upgrade the lighting in your home office, too. Your eyes will thank you. Use humidifiers, dehumidifiers, filters, purifiers, fans, air conditioners, and other machines to make breathing easier in your working space if you need to.

My Story about the Importance of Good Tools

Here's a personal story about the importance of having the right tools and the right support for those tools. I was having some connectivity issues with my work laptop. First, I had to make sure my internet connection was working. It took two days for my internet service provider to send a technician to my house and check my connection. It then took another day to find the real cause of the problem, which was a glitch with my wireless card on my laptop. It took the laptop's manufacturer another two days to ship the replacement part and have a technician come to my house to fix the laptop. Still, the problem was not solved. The new part unfortunately installed a wireless management software that conflicted with the native Windows wireless management software, and that also took another day to fix. Suffice it to say, had I been in the office, this issue which took six days to solve could have been fixed in one afternoon.

This issue could have taken a lot longer to fix than it did, were it not that my boss and IT department went the extra mile to make sure this problem was fixed, and they also took care of anything that needed to happen to help me recover happened.

The bottom line? Make sure you have the right tools, that these tools work properly, and that you and your company know what to do if those tools don't work properly.

13 - WORK LIFE BALANCE

"Happiness is not a matter of intensity but of balance, order, rhythm and harmony". - Thomas Merton

Being a telecommuter has many perks, and also many challenges. You will work harder and longer than some of your coworkers in the office just because you spend so much time in your office. You will find it harder to draw a clear line between your professional and personal lives. Finding balance in your life can be difficult, if not at times impossible. To achieve that balance, you need to set boundaries and establish solid precedents.

The first area in which you need to do this is in your professional relationships. Your coworkers and your other stakeholders (vendors, clients, etc...) need to know the timeframe within which they can expect you to be reachable and responsive. Keeping constant time habits allow them to plan accordingly. What this means for your own commitment is that during work hours, you give yourself fully to work and to nothing else. Work longer hours when it is needed to get the job done, but don't make it a regular habit. If you find this happening to you, chances are that you either have too much work to do, or that you're inefficient.

When you have created your routine and you are at work, be at work. Focus on work. Think of your time working at home as being the same as working in the office, and apply the same restrictions that you would have if you were in the office. For example, you wouldn't catch up on laundry or soap operas if you were in the office... Don't do it when you are in your home office.

Make sure you plan breaks and lunches the same way you do when you are in the office. Drive out of the house for lunch if necessary. Make yourself a sandwich in the morning or the night before, so you can enjoy them during your lunch breaks. Get your afternoon break, relax and get back to work. Keep your breaks short and use a timer if necessary to tell you to get back to work. Always being at home will drive you crazy. You need to get out of the house at least for a few minutes each day.

Keep in mind most people will think you are not really working when you are working at home. You need to remind everyone that working remotely is still working, which means you are not available during business hours.

Don't try to juggle work life and family life at the same time. Sometimes, even if you work at home, it may be a good idea to hire a babysitter or use a daycare service. You cannot be fully focused on your work and be fully focused on your family at the same time. The same goes for your pets. You do not want to be on a conference call and have your dog, cat, bird, or anteater make noises in the background, so you may need to arrange for pet care. The cost of daycare, babysitting, pet care, etc. may seem expensive to you, but you sometimes need to spend money in the short run to be more productive, and therefore earn more, in the long run.

14 - YOUR HEALTH

"It is health that is real wealth, not pieces of gold and silver" -
Mahatma Gandhi

Your health is perhaps your greatest asset. Staying
healthy is so important, and yet so hard to do. Here are
some tips to help you stay healthy as a telecommuter.

Get moving. Get at least 30 minutes of exercise every
day. Build exercise into your daily routine; for example,
place your printer at the far end of your office so that you
have to get up and walk to it. Consider taking short breaks
every few hours to breathe and stretch. Make your
workouts a to-do item in your schedule.

Eat smart. Nutrition is very important. You can't ask
your brain and body to give what you need if you don't
fuel up properly. Eat a balanced diet rich in fresh fruits and
vegetables, whole grains, and lean protein. Try to stay away
from processed foods. Drink water regularly, and limit
your caffeine intake. With your kitchen just a few steps
away, it's easy to eat more than you would at the office.
Many telecommuters gain weight because it's so easy to

snack throughout the day. Choose nuts, fruit, and cheese for healthy snacks, and limit your snack breaks.

Take time to take care of you. Many people make the mistake of rolling out of bed and working in their pajamas. As comfortable as that may seem, I know from experience you will feel more productive and energetic if you take a shower, get fully (but comfortably) dressed, and otherwise groom yourself as if you were going to work. Schedule regular medical, dental, and vision checkups. And don't forget to get enough sleep, either. Finally, schedule regular vacations and time away from work.

Get a grip on stress. Contrary to popular belief, telecommuting can be just as stressful as, if not more so, than working in the office. Meditation, yoga, and Tai Chi are helpful. Learn to delegate, and master the art of saying "no" to avoid spreading yourself too thin.

What about sick days? When people in the office get sick, they go work from home to remain productive while taking care of their health. What should you do if you already work from home and you get sick? Should you continue to work or should you call in sick? That depends on how you feel. If you truly don't think you are well enough to focus on work, then take a sick day. It's better to take a sick day than to perform poorly while working ill.

15 - YOUR DAILY ROUTINE - ONE DAY AT HOME WITH ME

"Amateurs sit and wait for inspiration, the rest of us just get up and go to work." - Stephen King

What is a day in the life of a telecommuter like? What might a day in your life look like? The most accurate answer I can give to these questions is "It depends." A typical day in your life does depend on many things, such as your industry, your company, your location, and many other factors. Perhaps the best way to answer that question is to give you a glimpse into a typical day in my life as a telecommuter. Obviously, your specific routine may vary, but I think my example will give you a good idea of what to expect when you telecommute.

Getting Off to a Good Start. So, what's a day in my life like? Actually, I start my day the night before. I make my personal to-do list for the day ahead and leave it on my desk at the end of the day. I make sure my Bible is by my comfy reading leather chair next to my prayer journal. I check on the battery life on my tablet and laptop, and make sure there are no dirty dishes in the kitchen to which

I will wake up the next morning. I grow lemon grass and other herbs in my vegetable garden, so I go out at night to pluck fresh leaves, wash them, and put them in the teapot, and add some cold water so that when I wake up, I just put the teapot on the stove to brew fresh herbal tea. I pick out my outfit for the next day too before getting in bed. While I lay in bed, I reprocess my entire day looking for things that I have done poorly, people I may have wronged, and blessings I may have overlooked. I make mental notes as to what I should do differently the next time similar situations occur. I usually fall asleep in the midst of these life adjustment plans.

I get on average three to four hours of sleep in the night. When I was in College, I held three jobs while taking eighteen credit hours in school, and I barely slept. That stage of my life has marked me permanently as I have not been able to sleep for extended hours ever since. When I wake up, I turn off the alarm on my cell phone, and look at my calendar on the phone while making mental notes of important events of the day.

After my morning shower, I get dressed, grab some tea and settle in my reading chair by the window for a few moments of meditation, reading, and prayers. This "quiet time" has been helpful when it comes to managing stress. I also take some time to spend a few minutes outside in my garden to get some Vitamin D in my system (living in Florida is a real plus, but you can find ways to get outdoors anywhere).

Getting Down to Business. After the transition to work, I get to my to-do list. I look through it and reconcile the to-dos with any emails that may have come in while I was away. I then "officially" start working. I draft all the emails that need to go out and send them out at about 9:00 AM. I've found that by blocking off certain segments of the day to handle email, I avoid the email "traffic jam" that plagues many workers. I am still growing in this area as I continue to get quite distracted by emails.

I usually start with a hard project and work on it until I get tired or stuck, and depending on how much time I have spent on it, I either take a break or turn to an easier task to keep my momentum going. I check my work and every project before I get started, when I am done with it, and before I send it out. The strategy around getting started with the most difficult task is to use all the energy on the project which will make the most impact. When you get stuck, you switch to an easy task in order to acquire a quick win. It would be the equivalent of a professional trapper/hunter who starts her day chasing down a lion, but by noon, she has not gotten a single kill yet. She shoots and kills a rabbit just to get a quick gain for the purse, and then get back on the lion's trail.

I often use a kitchen timer to keep me on task. My breaks throughout the day are limited to 15 minutes, and I take two to three such breaks, along with a 30-minute lunch. On my breaks, I set my timer for either 15 or 30 minutes, depending on whether it just a short break or a full lunch break. This time away from my work is very important to staying focused. Sometimes, I go for a 30-minute run on my lunch break, get back in the house, take a shower, and get back to work. I also set aside time for "administrative" activities such as booking an itinerary for business trips, completing timesheets, installing software, and other similar tasks. As I mentioned before, I block off segments of time to handle emails. So, at every hour (9:50, 11:50, etc...) I devote 10 minutes to emails and meeting invites.

If I need to spend time talking to people, I set up a block of time for that, so it doesn't interrupt my concentration. When I fall behind on work due to circumstances beyond my control, it takes time to get caught up, but I don't let myself feel discouraged. I push forward as hard as I can, ask for help when needed, and continue to make progress. If I have to be at a meeting or another event at a certain time, I use two timers. The first timer lets me know that it is getting close to the time I need to leave and gives me the opportunity to come to a stopping point. The second timer tells me to stop what I am doing and attend to that event.

Wrapping It Up. At the end of the work day, I update my to-do list for the next day and end the day on a positive note by taking some prayer time. I leave the house to attend one of my pre-scheduled post-work activities.

In order to get a good night's sleep, I take time to relax before going to bed, either by reading poetry, or watching some of the shows in my Hulu queue. When I am not too tired, I draw. In very busy times, I end up getting back to work from ten to midnight. I then take a break to read industry news and indulge in my social media network updates.

No matter how you choose to structure your work life, you need to find the approach that works for you and stick to it.

16 - YOUR PERSONAL FINANCES

"Rule#1: never lose money. Rule#2: don't forget rule #1." -
Warren Buffett

When you telecommute, you can save money in many areas. For one thing, you save on many expenses associated with commuting to work, such as gasoline, parking, tolls, bus/cab/train/subway fare, car maintenance, and even car insurance. You can also save by not having to buy an expensive work wardrobe that you'd wear in the office, not to mention dry cleaning it. You can reduce or even eliminate your need for child care. Plus, there are those "unexpected" expenses you don't have to worry about, like impromptu lunches, or dining out, or office gifts. Most importantly, telecommuting can be less stressful, which means better health and lower medical costs.

At the same time, there are areas in which you will spend more when you telecommute. Utilities are one such area, as you will simply use more water, heat, and electricity when you're at home—and don't forget the fact that you need faster phone and internet hookups, and you'll use them quite a bit too. You'll also need to purchase much of your office furniture and office supplies. And then there are those trips you take into the office, which could be everything from a few hours' drive or a cross-country flight.

To manage your spending as a telecommuter, follow these tips.

Track your expenses. Use Excel or other software to track all expenditures including non-reimbursed expenses. Check with your tax professional to find out if any of those expenses are tax-deductible.

Have a cash cushion. When it comes to travel or other work expenses, most companies will make you pay for your travel and work expenses, and then reimburse you. If you don't have a cushion in place, you will either run out of money or you will have to incur debts to cover these expenses while you wait to be reimbursed.

Don't spend the money you save too soon. You may be tempted to spend the money you save as a telecommuter on frivolities...Don't do it! While occasional splurges are acceptable, a great component of good wealth management is to spend less than you earn. Use those savings to your advantage by not wasting them.

Remember that time is money. Telecommuting also can give you more time, which can help you save money if you that time judiciously. For example cook your meal instead of dining out.

The bottom line? Have a plan for all of your spending, both business and personal, and stick to it.

17 - DON'T TAKE IT PERSONALLY

"I don't want to be at the mercy of my emotions. I want to use them, to enjoy them, and to dominate them." - Oscar Wilde

Your work is not you, but our society focuses a lot on work as part of our identity. Witness that when we meet someone new, one of the first questions we ask is "what do you do for a living?" We base so much of our identities on our work, but the healthiest approach here lies in four words: Don't take it personally.

This has been one of the hardest lessons for me to learn in my professional career. It's important to know that when a project you are leading fails, it does not translate into you being a failure. At the same time, you can be successful at work, yet still fail at the rest of your life.

In whatever industry you work in, there will be people who like your work, and there will be people who don't like it. Make your work excellent and unquestionable. Be proud of what you do, but never take it too personally. Keeping perspective helps you excel at taking constructive criticism, and incorporating it in your work without making it affect you spiritually. You will be able to stand behind your work and successfully defend your decisions inside and outside of your company, and most importantly, you will sleep well at night, and wake up the next morning to work another day knowing you did your best.

When you are in an office environment, and things go well (or not so well), you have others around you to celebrate with (or commiserate with), put ideas and thoughts together, and work through it. You can go to Happy Hour with some coworkers and talk through things. As a telecommuter, you live a work life that can be downright lonely. Plus, you are often "out of the loop" when it comes down to the office grapevine, so it's easy to fall into the trap of making assumptions, getting caught up in rumors, and assuming the worst.

So, what's a telecommuter to do? The bottom line is this: remember while your efforts are completely within your control, the outcome of your efforts often isn't. Factors like timing and luck often come into play with any success or failure. There are no guarantees in life, but there are ways to better your odds for success. Work is a big part of life, but it's only a part of your life.

18 - THE BOTTOM LINE

Love your work, but love yourself more. At the end of the day, you have to learn how to define success. What is success at work? What is success at home? Who are the stakeholders in your life?

You have heard many people say many times, things like "living with the end in mind," or "live as if today was your last day". They're regarded as clichés, but they are nevertheless true in their effect on our actions. At the 2005 Stanford commencement, Steve Jobs delivered an epic speech that has impacted people all over the world, and which resounds even more profound now that he is no longer with us. In the speech, he observed:

"Remembering that I'll be dead soon is the most important tool I've ever encountered to help me make the big choices in life. Because almost everything — all external expectations, all pride, all fear of embarrassment or failure — these things just fall away in the face of death, leaving only what is truly important. Remembering that you are going to die is the best way I know to avoid the trap of thinking you have something to lose. You are already naked. There is no reason not to follow your heart."

I have had the privilege to meet and know many successful individuals from many different walks of life. One commonality that transpires in all of them is that once you understand your finality and/or your purpose, all challenges and stormy days fade in the background of the journey of your life.

My best friend, to whom most of my happy memories in my teenage years are tied to, died this year. We are the same age, and to say that losing him troubled me is an understatement. In the midst of mourning this loss, I was brought back to another loss just a few years earlier. I buried my father in 2009, he died at age 52 of a massive heart attack. As I stood there staring down at his grave, I questioned the meaning of it all, and I told myself that at the end, when I lay in this very place, I want my resting place to read:

"Here lies Eryck Komlavi Dzotsi. The Lord was his passion, and with gladness he bore every cross he was given. He delighted in meekness. He was marked by forgiveness and known by his love. He was ruled by peace and fought the good fight... And he finished his course, a good and faithful servant."

With that mission in mind, when I started working from home, I faced every day, every task, and every challenge with the goal to finish the course as a good and faithful servant of my coworkers, my clients, my company, my family, my society, and God.

In order to achieve excellence as a telecommuter, or in any endeavor, remember honesty to yourself and a clear understanding of your purpose will be the foundation upon which the following elements will be built to create a stellar structure:

- Whom you are and what makes you happy
- Your company and their expectations
- Your commitment to your job
- Your ability to exceed your personal standards
- The application of your communication
- The relationship to your boss and teammates
- Your work environment and equipment
- Achieving and defending work-life balance
- Your family understanding of your work
- Planning and executing daily
- Your personal health and finances
- Putting your work in the proper perspective

Working remotely is a great experience, and there is no denying it carries many benefits:

- The ability to push yourself farther
- The freedom to work with more flexibility
- Less micro-management
- Less stress (if you do it right)
- Increased productivity
- A greater work/life balance
- Financial savings

The ultimate asset in your achievement of excellence while working remotely is none other than you. It is therefore my prayer as you finish this book, that you have read, understood, and put into practice the same strategies and tactics that have made me successful.

Remember that your success (or failure) in telecommuting is setting examples for others in your company. When you succeed as a telecommuter, you help build the case for others to telecommute. When you fail, managers who are reticent to allow their team members to work remotely find support for their reticence. So the next time you face a moment of tribulation and the choice between working hard and slacking off, between using time, money, and other resources frugally or profligately, remember that your choice, for good or ill, affects opportunities for others to telecommute.

Thank you for reading this book and I hope you have found it valuable. Thank you and God bless!

ABOUT ERYCK KOMLAVI DZOTSI

Eryck Komlavi Dzotsi is an experienced telecommuter with expertise in search engine optimization (SEO), social media marketing, and direct marketing. He has lent his expertise to leading organizations in their respective industries fields, including IMPAQT, the Embanet-Compass Group, Turnstile Publishing Company, Usbid.com, and ZoukStation.

Eryck has a Bachelor of Science degree in both Management Information Systems and Business Administration from the Florida Institute of Technology.

Born in the Republic of Togo, Eryck lived in many countries among which France, Ivory Coast, Ghana, and Benin prior to immigrating to the United States. He became a US citizen in 2012. Eryck is a man of Faith who is heavily involved in helping his community. He serves in different organizations in his hometown of Melbourne, Fl where he volunteers in ministries with focus on the poor, the homeless, the youth and the elderly.

REFERENCES

Watkins, Michael (2003) The First 90 Days: Critical Success Strategies for New Leaders at All Levels - (Harvard Business Review Press)

International Data Corporation -
http://www.idc.com/getdoc.jsp?containerId=232073

Mashable Magazine
http://mashable.com/2011/04/06/train-remote-employees/

Steve Jobs' 2005 Stanford commencement
http://news.stanford.edu/news/2005/june15/jobs-061505.html